This fun **Phonics** reader

belongs to

_____

Ladybird Reading

Phonics

BOOK **9**

Contents

A catalogue record for this book is available from the British Library

Published by Ladybird Books Ltd
80 Strand London WC2R 0RL
A Penguin Company

2 4 6 8 10 9 7 5 3 1
© LADYBIRD BOOKS LTD MMVI
LADYBIRD and the device of a Ladybird are trademarks of Ladybird Books Ltd

Printed in China

Baboon on the Moon

by Mandy Ross
illustrated by John-Paul Early

introducing the common spellings of the long **u** sound, as in moon, few and blue

u-e

oo

June the baboon wanted to go to the moon.

She tried to get there on a moon scooter.

But the scooter blew up with a boom!

Next, June tried to swoop to the moon in a big blue balloon.

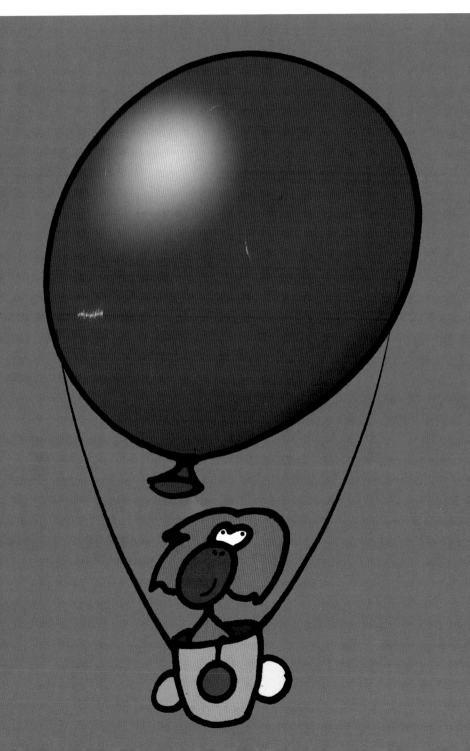

OO

Soon the balloon came down.

I feel a fool!

Then June the baboon got some Groovy Zoom Boots.

**She swooped and
she looped,**

as she flew through the gloom.

And June the baboon flew right to the moon.

Sir Skylight

by Mandy Ross

illustrated by Cecilia Johansson

introducing the common spellings of the long **i** sound, as in high, lie and sky

This is Sir Skylight. He is a shining white knight.

He is brave in the daytime,

but not at night.

igh

He fights with all his might when there is sun and lots of light.

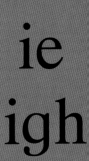

Yet he flies home in fright
whenever it is night.

Sir Skylight's mum comes
to tuck him up tight,

but he lies and he sighs
and he cries all night.

Then Sir Skylight has a bright idea…

NEW!
KNIGHT-
LIGHTS
For night
riding.

"I'll be alright at night with these nice bright lights," he says.

So now when the moon shines brightly in the sky,

Sir Skylight rides round with his head held high.

Zoot Scoot Boogie Woogie

by Mandy Ross
illustrated by Stephen Holmes

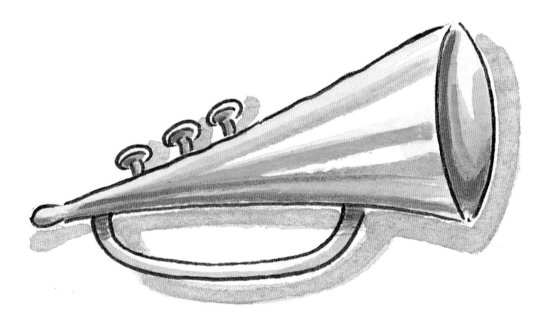

to practise the common spellings of the long **a** , **e** , **i** , **o** and **u** sounds

o-e

The animals are on the move
with a hurry and scurry.

Jake Snake and Wayne
Whale take the train.

Peter Cheetah pushes Neil Seal in his green wheelbarrow.

Mike Tiger and Kyle Crocodile
ride their sky-bike.

Now we're flying!

oa
oe
o-e
ow

Joan Goat and Joel Mole
go by rowing boat.

Row,
slowcoach, row!

June Baboon and
Sue Kangaroo use their
Groovy Zoom Boots.

ay
ey

The animals all hurry and scurry, for today is the day they are going to play…

in the Zoot Scoot Boogie Woogie Animal Band!

HOW TO USE
Phonics
BOOK 9

This book introduces the common spellings of the long u and i vowel sounds. The fun stories will help your child begin reading words including any of the several spelling patterns that represent these sounds.

- Read each story through to your child first. Familiarity helps children identify some of the words and phrases.

- Have fun talking about the sounds and pictures together – what repeated sound can your child hear in each story?

- Help your child break new words into separate sounds (eg. m-oo-n) and blend their sounds together to say the word.

- Some words, such as 'come', 'move' and even 'the', can't be read by sounding out. Help your child practise recognising words like these.

- **Baboon on the Moon and Sir Skylight**

  Talk about the letter groups as outlined on the title page of each story. There are also instances of the 'magic e' spelling pattern, covered in detail in Book 7.

Phonic fun

Zoot Scoot Boogie Woogie

This story offers your child a chance to revise all five of the long vowel sounds, in the various spellings introduced in Books 7, 8 and 9.

Ladybird Reading

Phonics

Phonics is part of the Ladybird Reading range. It can be used alongside any other reading programme, and is an ideal way to practise the reading work that your child is doing, or about to do in school.

Ladybird has been a leading publisher of reading programmes for the last fifty years. **Phonics** combines this experience with the latest research to provide a rapid route to reading success.

The fresh quirky stories in Ladybird's twelve **Phonics** storybooks are designed to help your child have fun learning the relationship between letters, or groups of letters, and the sounds they represent.

This is an important step towards independent reading – it will enable your child to tackle new words by sounding out and blending their separate parts.

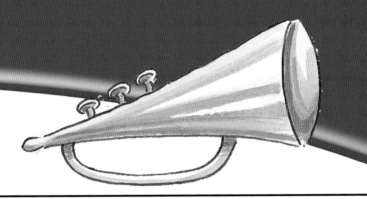

How Phonics works

- The stories and rhymes introduce the most common spellings of over 40 key sounds, known as phonemes, in a step-by-step way.

- Rhyme and alliteration (the repetition of an initial sound) help to emphasise new sounds.

- Bright amusing illustrations provide helpful picture clues and extra appeal.